My First Trip

to the

USS Yorktown

in

Charleston Harbor

Lane W. Russell

To order additional copies of this book, contact:
Xlibris
844-714-8691
www.Xlibris.com
Orders@Xlibris.com

ISBN: Softcover   978-1-6698-5878-2
               Hardcover   978-1-6698-5879-9
               EBook   978-1-6698-5877-5

Print information available on the last page

Rev. date: 12/15/2022

Dedicated to those that served and serve.

This is my trip to the USS Yorktown.

On August 11, 2022 my Gaga and Papa surprised me with a trip to Patriots Point at Charleston Harbor to see the USS Yorktown.

First, I went on a two-hour trip and I saw a big aircraft carrier, the name of it is the USS Yorktown.

Second, before going on the aircraft carrier I was able to climb on a big gun. I am not sure what the name of it was.

I was so excited as we walked the bridge toward the carrier! This was the most amazing trip ever!

Before we went in the Yorktown, I got my picture by a big "I Pledge Allegiance" sign. The sun was so bright that I had to cover my eyes.

Before entering the ship there were several bronze plaques that tell a lot about the Yorktown, and dedicated to all that served on her.

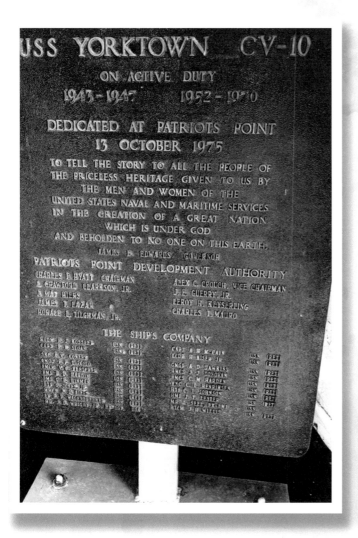

We met a veteran who served in the Air Force during Vietnam. He showed pictures of tankers refueling fighters in the air with the boom. This was so awesome!

Next, was my very favorite, getting to see the Medal of Honor rooms. The first picture was that of the youngest Medal of Honor recipient. He was a drummer boy in the Civil War and only 12-years-old.

I was awestruck reading and seeing all of the pictures. No one talked in the rooms as if to preserve their memory.

Next, we went down in the hull of the ship and saw the bathrooms. One picture shows my Papa coming around the corner, but he didn't use a toilet as they are not functional.

I then got to sit in a dental chair. I wonder how many soldiers sat there in all the years.

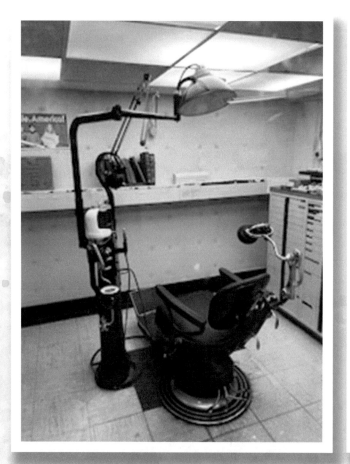
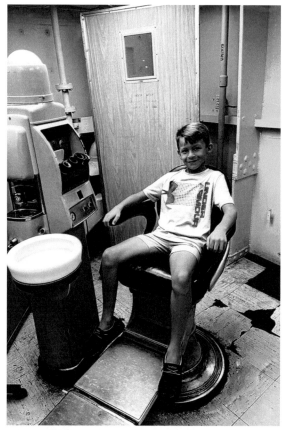

I had my picture taken with a couple of airmen in a cut-out.

I was telling my Gaga and Papa about the ropes and hooks on the planes, and how this helped the planes stop. They are called the arresting wires and tailhooks.

The flight deck was next. This was so awesome!! There are all different types of aircraft up there. Gaga took a picture of Papa and me at one of the ends. It would be scary not to have a fence around it. One guide told us that the sailors would sleep on the flight deck because it would get really hot.

In this picture, Papa is showing me Fort Sumter out in the water where the first shot of the Civil War was fired.

I wanted to go on this submarine, Clamagore, but it was being prepared to get towed away to be used for scrap metal. So sad.

Finally, I got to sit in the Commander's chair. Amazing!

I got to check out controls, turn the wheels, radar, and see all the levels and how the soldiers and sailors lived and worked.

My Gaga and I got to ride in a simulator. That was fun, but not too realistic I don't think.

Next, we got to board the Destroyer USS Laffey. A guide told us the history of the Laffey. It was hit by kamikazies. The guide said the Laffey is the most decorated WWII destroyer in existence. Sad to think of all the dead and wounded that happened there.

On the Laffey is this remote controlled drone that was used to sink Japanese submarines. That was one of the most amazing things to hear about and see.

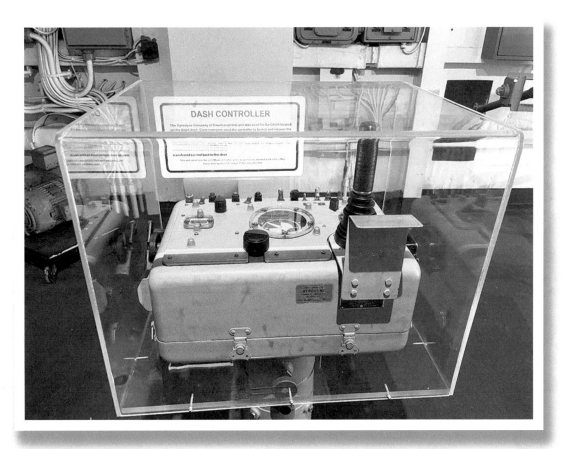

After the Laffey, we walked over to the Vietnam Experience. This had actual aircraft, patrol boat, and tanks with all the sounds of Vietnam. It sounded so real. In one of the huts we got to watch a short movie about Vietnam. My Gaga told me how the Vietnamese would hide in tunnels.

That is the end of my trip. I already look forward to getting to go back to Patriots Point and get to see Fort Sumter too.

The End.

Printed in the United States
by Baker & Taylor Publisher Services